Quipu

ALSO BY ARTHUR SZE

The Willow Wind
(1972; revised, 1981)

Two Ravens
(1976; revised, 1984)

Dazzled (1982)

River River (1987)

Archipelago (1995)

The Redshifting Web:
Poems 1970–1998 (1998)

The Silk Dragon:
Translations from the Chinese (2001)

QUIPU

Arthur Sze

Copper Canyon Press

Copper Canyon Press is in residence at Fort Worden State Park
in Port Townsend, Washington, under the auspices of Centrum Foundation.
Centrum is a gathering place for artists and creative thinkers from around
the world, students of all ages and backgrounds, and audiences seeking
extraordinary cultural enrichment.

LIBRARY OF CONGRESS CATALOGING-IN-PUBLICATION DATA

Sze, Arthur.
Quipu / Arthur Sze.
p.   cm.
ISBN 1-55659-226-4 (pbk: alk. paper)
I. Title.
PS3569.Z38Q57 2005
811'.54 – DC22   2005008864

COPPER CANYON PRESS
Post Office Box 271
Port Townsend, Washington 98368

www.coppercanyonpress.org

For Carol

ACKNOWLEDGMENTS

Grateful acknowledgment is made to the editors of the following publications in which these poems, sometimes in earlier versions, first appeared:

Boston Review: "Aqueous Gold," "Thermodynamics"

The Butcher Shop: "Acanthus"

Carnet de Route (Paris): "The Angle of Reflection Equals the Angle of Incidence"

Chicago Review: "The Angle of Reflection Equals the Angle of Incidence," "Haircutting"

Conjunctions: "Earthshine," "Quipu"

Dimsum (Hong Kong): "Earthshine"

The Drunken Boat (online): "Earthstar," "Spring Smoke"

Field: "Oracle-Bone Script," "X and O"

The Iowa Review: "Ox-Head Dot," "Syzygy"

Jubilat: "The Welt"

The Kenyon Review: "Before Sunrise," "Didyma," "Lobed Bowl with Black Glaze and White Scalloped Rim"

Mānoa: "Acanthus," "The Chromatics of Dawn," "In the Living Room," "Inflorescence," "Spring Smoke"

Orion: "Earthstar"

Unitas (Taipei): "Lobed Bowl with Black Glaze and White Scalloped Rim"

Washington Square: "Solstice Quipu"

Xcp: Cross Cultural Poetics: "Ice Line," "The Thermos"

The Best American Poetry 2004 (Scribner): "Acanthus"

In Company: An Anthology of New Mexico Poets After 1960 (University of New Mexico Press): "Ox-Head Dot"

Inscriptions in the Starry Sky (Taiwan Cultural Affairs Bureau): "Lobed Bowl with Black Glaze and White Scalloped Rim," translated into Chinese by Chen Li

Photographers, Writers, and the American Scene: Visions of Passage (Arena Editions): "Before Sunrise," "Earthshine," "Earthstar," "Haircutting," "La Bajada"

The Poet's Child (Copper Canyon Press): "The Thermos"

Wild and Whirling Words (Etruscan Press): "Ox-Head Dot"

The Wisdom Anthology of North American Buddhist Poetry (Wisdom Publications): "Before Sunrise," "In the Living Room," "Inflorescence," "Solstice Quipu," "Thermodynamics"

"Before Sunrise" appeared as a Dia Center for the Arts broadside; "Earthshine," as a letterpress book from Felix Press; "Earthstar," as a Felix Press broadside; and "Spring Smoke," as a Folger Shakespeare Library broadside.

I wish to thank the Lila Wallace–Reader's Digest Fund and the National Millennium Survey for their support.

Contents

vii

Quipu

QUIPU \\'kē-(,)pü\\ *n* [Sp *quipo*, fr. Quechua *khipu*] (1704): a device made of a main cord with smaller varicolored cords attached and knotted and used by the ancient Peruvians (as for calculating)

— Merriam-Webster's Collegiate Dictionary

Before Sunrise

The myriad unfolds from a progression of strokes –
one, ice, corpse, hair, jade, tiger.

Unlocking a gate along a barbed-wire fence,
I notice beer cans and branches in the acequia.

There are no white pear blossoms by the gate,
no red poppies blooming in the yard,

no *Lepiota naucina* clustered by the walk,
but – bean, gold – there's the intricacy of a moment

when – wind, three-legged incense cauldron –
I begin to walk through a field with cow pies

toward the Pojoaque River, sense deer, *yellow*, rat.
I step through water, go up the arroyo, find

a dark green magpie feather. This is a time
when – blood in my piss, ache in nose and teeth –

I sense tortoise, flute where there is no sound,
wake to human bones carved and strung into a loose apron.

Earthshine

"Fuck you, *fuck you*," he repeated as he drove down the dirt road
    while tamarisk branches scraped the side of the pickup;

      what scrapes in the mind as it dilates to darkness?

    "*Jodido*," he winced and turned up the whites of his eyes;

      "What comes from darkness, I strike with darkness";

        who hears a night-blooming cereus
      unfold a white blossom by the windowsill?

      crackle of flames in the fireplace;

        lapping of waves against rocks
      as a manta ray flips and feeds on plankton;

    the gasp when he glanced down at the obituaries;

the gasp when she unwrapped flecked rice paper to find a letterpress broadside;

    spurt of match into gold as he lights white beeswax candles;

      she is running her hair between his toes;
      he is rubbing her nipples with his palms;

    "What comes from brightness, I strike with brightness";

    his ankles creaked as he tiptoed to the bathroom;

    waking to a cat chewing on a mouse in the dark.

Hiking up a trail in the Manoa Valley arboretum,
he motions with his hand to stop as he tries
to distinguish whether a red-whiskered or
red-vented bulbul has just landed on a branch.
I spot a macadamia nut on the ground, glance
up into an adjacent tree and am shocked by
two enormous jackfruit suspended from the trunk.
Revelation never comes as a fern uncoiling
a frond in mist; it comes when I trip on a root,
slap a mosquito on my arm. We go on, but stop
when gnats lift into a cloud as we stumble into
a bunch of rose apples rotting on the ground.
Although we continue to a dead end where water
runs down a sheer rock, the mind stops here:
here *Amanita muscarias* release a cloud of spores
into cool August air; here lovers make
earthshine on a waxing crescent moon; here
the phone rings and I learn of a suicide,
a pinhole grows into an eclipse; here
water drips as I descend into a sloping black lava tube.

3

Say teeth;
say gnawed his teeth in his sleep;
say each spring he scraped peeling blue paint off the windowsill;
say the ocean flickers;
say a squiggly chalk line screeching down a blackboard opens a black rift;
say on a float house yellow cedar smoke rises in the woodstove;
say burn;
say crumpled white papers ripple then burst into yellow twists of flame;
say parallel lines touch in the infinite;
say peel;
say stoplight screech go green laugh;
say screech, rip, slam, thud, body scrapes, bleeds to bone;
say hyena;
say bobcat stripped of skin;
say a black cricket chirps in a corner of the room;
say hang;
say ox shoulder hangs off hook;
say trimming roses, she slashed her left wrist;
say shit-smear hair-sway leaf-gold ooze;
say crack;
say breaking a wineglass in a white napkin recovers a sliver of original light;
say egg-white eyeball splash;
say rinse;
say bend to earth, find a single stalk budding gold.

4

He hanged himself with his belt in the bosque
is no longer a whip that reddens and flays the skin.
"Donkey piss," he once cracked – but who
knows how the light sizzled and burned a hole
that gnawed and gnawed so that the more he
twisted the more he convulsed into a black pitch?
Orange daylilies are blooming along the driveway;
long-stalked delphiniums are bending to earth.
A firework explodes in white gold then bursts
into a green shimmer. He leaves teeth marks
on her neck; she groans and shows the whites
of her eyes. When a car rushes by on a wet road,
he hears a laborer throw sand against a tilted screen
and realizes twenty-three years ago he threw
sand against a tilted screen. Now, when he
strokes the tendons of her left wrist, she sighs.
They are now nowhere everywhere nonesuch;
they are not *look back time* but full moon first light.

5

She said he said "moon" in his sleep;

when he looked through the potbellied telescope,
the light of the full moon made him wince;

he had to gaze into darkness
and then saw from Mare Cognitum to Mare Serenitatis;

the mind aches to see at such distance such definition;

when she heard the barking dog,
she shined a flashlight and spotted a porcupine on the roof;

as you would spotlight a deer;

a snake slides under the redwood boardwalk by the kitchen;

he kisses her shoulders,
rubs the soles of her feet;

the mind aligns such slivers;

say dragonfly, quartz, cattail, tuning fork, wave;
say earthstar bursting into alpine air;
say c^2;

say even the sacred barley drink separates if it is not stirred,
and see how, stirred, one can find repose.

6

Sipping mint tea in the ebbing heat of the day,
I recollect how we stumbled onto a raccoon
squashed between boards leaning against a fence,
tadpoles wriggling at the edge of a pond.
On the living-room table, thirty-six peonies
in a vase dry and become crepe-paper light
to touch. Yesterday you watered blue chamisa
along the county road, while I watered desert grass
under the willow. I recollect opening a brown,
humid box and, stunned, lifted a handful
of morels, inhaling the black aroma of earth.
What is it we give each other – gold, shark's fin –
other than a renewed sense of the miraculous?
Nanao watched a blip on the radar screen; later,
when he saw the flash, he thought Mt. Fuji
had erupted in a burst of light. Sipping mint tea
on the longest day of the year, I sense how
the balance of a life sways, and a petal may tip it.

7

A steady evening with a first-quarter moon;
numerous craters along the terminator are razor sharp;

I observe the ghostly bluish glow of earthshine
and feel how the moon has no permanent dark side.

A horse neighs by the barbed-wire fence;
we trudge into a wet field, carrying, from under the portal,

a bee's nest in a basket, place it in a nook
of a silver poplar. Will any bees hatch in spring?

I notice thorns on the bare branches of Russian olives;
you spot coyote scat before the V-shaped gate.

We walk to where the Pojoaque and Nambe flow together –
I am amazed at how we blossom into each other.

I hear the occasional drone of cars on Highway 285,
hear how the living expire into smoke

and the dead inflame the minds of the living.
When I exhale against a cold window, I see

the ever-shifting line along the terminator;
and, as the shadow cast by the rim of Theophilus

slips across the crater's floor, I feel light
surge into a honeycomb gold – it all goes and comes at once.

Ox-Head Dot

Ox-head dot, wasp waist, mouse tail,
bamboo section, water-caltrop, broken branch,
stork leg, a pole for carrying fuel:
these are the eight defects when a beginning
calligrapher has no bone to a stroke.

I have no names for what can go wrong:
peeling carrots, a woman collapses
when a tumor in her kidney ruptures;
bronze slivers from a gimbal nut
jam the horizontal stabilizer to a jet,

make it plunge into the Pacific Ocean;
"Hyena!" a man shouts into the darkness
and slams shut the door. Stunned, I hear
a scratching, know that I must fumble,
blunder, mistake, fail; yet, sometimes

in the darkest space is a white fleck,
ox-head dot; and when I pass through,
it's a spurt of match into flame,
glowing moths loosed into air, air
rippling, roiling the surface of the world.

Syzygy

I notice headlights out the living-room window
then catch the bass in a pickup as it drives by.
I am shocked to learn that doctors collected
the urine of menopausal nuns in Italy to extract
gonadotropins. And is that what one draws,
in infinitesimal dose, out of a vial?
I remember a steel-wool splinter in my finger
and how difficult it was to discern, extract
under a magnifying glass; yet – blue mold,
apple dropping from branch – it is hard to see
up close when, at the periphery, the unexpected
easily catches the eye. Last Thursday night,
we looked through binoculars at the full moon,
watched it darken and darken until, eclipsed,
it glowed ferrous-red. By firelight, we glowed;
my fingertips flared when I rubbed your shoulders,
softly bit your ear. The mind is a tuning fork
that we strike, and, struck, in the syzygy
of a moment, we find the skewed, tangled
passions of a day begin to straighten, align, hum.

La Bajada

Driving north before Cochiti exit, he visualizes
a bleeding anthropologist pulled from a wrecked car

but encounters only starlight and wind. Tonight
cars glide past him at eighty. Marine biologists

believed the coelacanth was extinct until a fisherman
off Madagascar pulled one up in a net. After 40,000

photographs in a bubble chamber, technicians had no track
of omega minus and wanted to quit. Sometimes luck

and sometimes perseverance. In the morning he stirred
to agapanthus odor, felt presence and absence

resemble an asymptotic line and curve that squeeze
closer and closer but do not touch. He glances up

at Cassiopeia arcing toward the north-northwest,
wonders if mosquito eggs in the pond are about to hatch,

sees her trim red and orange ranunculi on the counter.
And as he pushes on the gas and begins to ascend

La Bajada, water runs in the acequia
behind the kitchen porch for the first time this year.

Spring Smoke

The minutes ooze into a honeycomb gold.
He reads in a recently discovered notebook

that in 1941 his grandfather refused
to collaborate with the puppet government

and was kidnapped in Shanghai, held
in a smoky loft where he breathed

through a hole in the roof while his captors
unloaded, reloaded revolvers, played

mahjong. He pauses to adjust the light,
wonders if the wasp nest lodged on a beam

in the shed is growing. His grandfather
describes a woman who refused to divulge

where her husband was until they poured
scalding tea down her throat and crushed

her right hand in a vise. He glances up
but cannot discern stars through the skylight.

He senses smoky gold notes rising
out of a horn and knows how easy it is

to scald, blister, burst. This morning
when he drew back a wood slat

to swing the gate, he glimpsed a young
pear tree blossoming in the driveway.

Haircutting

She snips his hair with new scissors.
He ponders rain on the skylight, x^x,

his father sent him an elephant tusk
carved into a village with lotus ponds

and waterfalls. His son, asleep, left
on the kitchen table in an unwaxed bag

clusters of chanterelles. Who probes
for ice crystals below the moon's surface?

He recalls a physicist who loved to raft
the Taos Box, complained of recurring

headaches, had a stroke, died. She is
wearing a string of graduated pearls

with a jade clasp. He puts his hands
on her hips, savors unbuttoning her blouse.

When a letter from Peter arrived today,
he slit it open: violin, *jarana*, harp music

from La Sierra de Zongolica spilled out.
In the aftermath of a miscarriage,

she loops back to a moonrise over White Sands,
to a skunkbush sumac in a transverse dune.

Lobed Bowl with Black Glaze and White Scalloped Rim

Turning from the obituary page,
he hears a screw tighten,
recalls a dead sparrow on a greenhouse floor.

The mind can be dipped in a vat
when you slice an eggplant, sharpen a pencil,
shave. He woke slowly as light

sank through the skylight, brightening
the bedroom. He recalls running
his tongue from her breast to her armpit

as she shivered with pleasure.
An elder holds an eagle feather,
wafts cedar smoke, taps a woman

on her shoulders. He wants a mind
as pure as a ten-lobed bowl
with black glaze and white scalloped rim.

A broad-tailed hummingbird whirs in the air —
and in a dewdrop on a mimosa leaf
is the day's angular momentum.

Quipu

I try to see a bald eagle nest in a Douglas fir
but catch my sleeve on thorns, notice blackberries,

hear large wings splashing water in a lagoon.
I glimpse a heron perched on a post above a tidal flat,

remember red elderberries arcing along a path
where you catch and release a newt among ferns.

And as a doe slips across the road behind us,
we zigzag when we encounter a point of resistance,

zigzag as if we describe the edge of an immense leaf,
as if we plumb a jagged coastline where tides

wash and renew the mind. I stare at abalone eyes,
am startled at how soft a sunflower star is to touch,

how sticky a tentacle of an anemone is to finger.
When we walk barefoot in sand, I sway

to the motion of waves, mark bits of crabs
washed to shore, see – in an instant a dog wrenches

a leash around the hand of a woman, shatters bones –
ensuing loss salamanders the body, lagoons the mind.

Here a red horse leaned over a barbed-wire fence
and uprooted a row of corn; here chili plants
rotted after a thunderstorm; here the force of rain
exposed carrot seeds and washed almost all away;
but here two kinds of eggplants flower in a row;

here peas, cucumbers, bell peppers, eggplants,
tomatoes, melons, corn. Is this wave of flowering
the arc of loss? She closes her eyes and aches:
in a white room, the ultrasound picks up yolk sac
and curled embryo: inside the space of a pea,

a head, mouth, neural tube, brain stem, eyes;
but it does not pulse or flicker with a heartbeat.
Across the room, they reach out, but to what?
The room darkens as the screen ionizes, glows.
He visualizes a series of photographic still lifes:

polished tin doorknob against a black background,
whale vertebra seen from afar against a black background,
nineteen stacked pancakes against a black background,
cluster of hazelnuts up close against a black background;
and suddenly when he opens his eyes, he cannot hear.

3

Who touched a quipu and made it explode into dust?

What blooms as briefly as scarlet gaura in sandy soil?

How incandescent is a grief?

Did spun wool delineating the corn of the Incas obliterate in a second?

What incipient white fades into pink?

Did the knots of her loves jaguar in an instant?

What is the tensile strength of a joy?

Who observed a great horned owl regurgitate bones into the arroyo?

What hides in the wave of a day?

A single blue unknotted cord – what does it mean?

How can the mind ply the forms of desire?

From south to north, east to west: which length is greater?

When is a koan not a koan?

Who can unravel the spin of an elegy and counterspin it into an ode?

Who whispered, "as is"?

Where is a passion that orchids the body?

Whose carded cotton fibers are these?

4

7:14: red numbers on the clock incarnadine the time;
he stares at the maroon jar of a kerosene lamp,
the carmine batik hanging under a skylight.

And when he drives home, the red at the stop sign
is the bright red blood on a sheet;
yet candles in the living room conjure bliss.

He has the urge to stroll down to a spring-fed pond
where he sits on a rusted bench, stares into water;
tiny fish dart near; a green frog lifts its head;

then a vermilion dragonfly hovers near irises,
zigzags back and forth as it weaves an invisible web.
He guesses it eats mosquitoes and midges, though

he can only catch sunlight glint off its wings.
The mind zigzags back – swimming in a tidal pond,
they brushed jellyfish with their arms and legs –

loops a red cord that records loss and loss.
When he trudges back and closes his eyes,
he is startled by a cricket chirping in the fireplace.

5

When he opened the book to the page with *quipu*,
he glimpsed, through the underside of the sheet,

the image of a quince. Sometimes the thing you want
bleeds *in* the light. When yellow leaves dropped

off the cottonwood, he spotted, up high, a large nest
and a magpie hopping from branch to branch.

When he stubbed his toe in the dark, he flashed
on how he dug his first matsutake out of the dirt,

fingered brown scales on the cap and stalk.
Now, as he stares into her eyes, she relates how

two men, rescued in the Andes, suffered frostbite:
one had his arms and legs amputated but is now

moving with artificial limbs, while the other,
who tried to hold on to his extremities, suffers

in a wheelchair. When she says, "I don't want
to become *that*," the *no* smears fingerprints on glass.

And he sees a man splashed with blood and scales
stand hip deep in halibut, cleaning them off.

6

Who has heard a flute carved from the wing bone of a crane?

they hung tomato plants upside down in the kitchen;

a dyer poured fermented piss into the dye bath;

explosion of egg and sperm;

a hummingbird nest tucked in some branches
tucked in his mind;

she groaned when he yanked her hair back;

inside the space of a pea,
beginningless beginning and endless end;

he diverts water from the acequia, irrigates slender peach trees;

when he pulled the skeins up,
they gasped when they turned blue in the air;

they folded an ultrasound image inside a red envelope with a white crane,
prayed, set it on fire;

he wove a blue jaguar;

plucking ripened tomatoes, she grazed shriveled leaves;

"All men are mortal";

they prayed to the sun, burned the blue jaguar at noon;

conception: 186,000 miles per second;

186,000 miles per second;

who has heard a flute carved from the wing bone of a crane?

7

Crows pick at a dead buffalo along the curve
of the river, as Raz trots up with a cow hoof

in his mouth. As: to the same degree or amount;
for instance; when considered in a specified

form or relation; in or to the same degree
in which; as if; in the way or manner that;

in accordance with what or the way in which;
while, when; regardless of the degree to which;

for the reason that; that the result is.
As in a quipu where colored, knotted strings

hang off a primary cord – or as a series
of acequias off the Pojoaque River drop water

into fields – the mind ties knots, and I
follow a series of short strings to a loose end –

stepping barefoot in white sand, rolling
down a dune, white flecks on our lips,

on our eyelids, sitting in a warm dune
as a gibbous moon lifts against the sky's pelagic,

with the shadows of fourwing saltbushes,
the scent of hoary rosemarymint in the air.

8

I close my eyes — fishhooks and nylon threads
against a black background, cuttlefish
from above against a black background,

blowfish up close against a black background.
The seconds are as hushed as the morning
after steady snowfall when the power is out,

the rooms cold. At one, a snow-heavy branch
snapped the power line; the loose end flailed
clusters of orange sparks. A woman swept

a walkway, missed a porch step, fell forward,
bruised her face, broke both elbows; yet
the body quickens in the precarious splendor

that *it would not be better if things happened
to men just as they wish,* that — moonglow,
sunrise — the day — scales of carp in frost on glass —

scalds and stuns. In 1,369 days, we've set
eagle to eagle feather and formed a nest
where — fishhook joy — the mind is new each day.

9

We bend to enter a cave at Tsankawi, inadvertently
stir some tufa dust, notice it catches a beam

of sunlight. The beam enters a ceiling shaft
at winter solstice noon and forms, on a plastered wall,

a slash, then a small circle of intense light
before it disappears. And when we leave,

you sizzle with the vanished point of light.
I sizzle when I remember how we first kissed,

when I ran my hands along your shoulders,
when you brushed lashes on my neck. And as flying

geese cast shadows on water, and water reflects
the light, a joy stretches and stretches

into the infinite. I recall when we knocked at
our neighbors' door to drop off a gift, how

they didn't hear us as they were staring out
at the feeder counting birds – bushtit, sapsucker,

nuthatch, woodpecker – as we counted the blessing
of seconds where heat shimmered and vanished into air.

Aqueous Gold

1

At six A.M., the Big Dipper has swung overhead;
in an hour you will look up to rose-tinged
cirrus clouds. When I shut my eyes, waves
unfurl; I rouse to cries of birds before
sunrise, recall the imprint of our bodies
in white sand; from the beach, water deepens
into teal blue in no time. Aqueous gold
ripples on the surfaces of waves, but when
you reach for it there, it is here, and
when you reach for it here, it vanishes.
The mind craves to make something perdurable
out of something as tenuous as candlelight,
something that becomes more and more itself
through vicissitude. When a selenographer
plots the moon's seas, does he inscribe
a memory that can batter as well as renew?
We kindle into flame a firelight by which
we incandesce more and more of ourselves.
Inscribed in the motion of birth and death,
we poise, savor the resistance to move too soon.

2

In the impoverishment of memory, you listen
to a cricket crawl in a pipe below the sink
but cannot see it, finger a cracked vase,
yet treasure its sliver of death. When you
reach out to touch a woman on her deathbed,
the flush of her skin is no longer a surprise:
eyes closed, absorbing oxygen through a tube,
she will never hate, love, sing, connive,
speak, stir again. In a barrio apartment,
you pull on a light: cockroaches flick
their forelegs and snap flat their forewings.
You listen to the drone of a refrigerator,
drips from faucets. In a Ketchikan bar,
a man trembles and recounts how a bear swiped
his right eye, how the eye ran like raw egg,
though you surmise he moves from bar to bar
to repeat his pain. You step out into drizzle:
the snow line has dropped to eighty feet
above the docks. Thoughts inch through
memory the way maggots inch through a cèpe.

3

A candle undulates on the mantel; at the end
of winter, water in the pond is clear with
twig and leaf debris clumped at the bottom.
They yearn for an instant that clears the mind;
in the warm yellow light at their fingertips,
they sense what dies is cast into the molten
form of the moment, as prayers are tossed
into the molten cast of a bell: *yellow,*
this, sun, wet, shudder, shriek, torque, be.
Though a potter can remove with tongs a molten
bowl out of a kiln, plunge it into water,
they have nothing but a snake of words
to prove this moment when a chrysanthemum
unfolds in steaming broth in a black bowl;
when it heats, warms their hands; when they
recognize a pale green leaf is beginning
to flare out; apple tree beginning to bud;
when a sliver of moon begins to widen;
when they quiver and end this stillness,
begin to stretch into another glistening stillness.

4

Tying a balloon to the zoo's iron gate, he catches
the blink of a cashier before she rings
up another fee, hungers for the moment a turtle
slips into water. Inside, he pauses at a tank,
views nothing, puts his hands on glass; at once
a phalanx of piranhas veers and repels light.
He studies their glistening jaws, eyes, incisors,
turns to a peacock pacing back and forth
on the floorboards, scarlet ibises with folded wings.
A single loss can ravel the mind with grief
and – meteor shower – hours days minutes seconds –
make us reach for white narcissi by the window
at sunrise. In the park, crimson and orange
oak leaves burn into transparency: is a moment
of death a seed? A friend once ignited fireworks
over a dry lake to tremble what expires
and what persists: streaming red gossamers,
yellow showers, violet chrysanthemums arcing
into gold into black air. Bending to tie a shoelace,
he confronts pocked craters in the irregular asphalt.

5

In a few minutes the sky lightens so that
branches of the willow flare to the very twig.
The hiss when a molten bowl is plunged into water
is also the hiss when you ladle water onto rocks
in the sauna. It is not in the hoofprints of zebras
or in the shadows of oryxes, but in the scent
of a lynx by a goose pen. The warmth and aroma of wax
in this flickering room is not to be inscribed
on papyrus wrapped around a corpse, nor is it
currency to be burned into the next fearless world.
It is when we true ourselves to the consequence
that we find the yellow lightning of our kiss.
Though we sit inscribed in a circle, we twist
and smell a wild fennel stalk in our hands.
Moose calves with dangling wet umbilical cords
struggle to keep up with their long-legged fast-
moving mothers. Ascending a series of wooden steps,
we gaze down, and, as large multicolored koi
leisurely swim in the pool below, one koi
flaps and shivers gold flecks onto the surface.

6

Clusters of wild irises shrivel in the field.
He tries to slide the ring off his mother's
finger, but rigor mortis has set in; he soaps
her finger, swivels the ring, yanks it off.
I catch the motion with which a man tosses
water from a brush onto a setting cement curb,
while another trowels the cement to an olive shine.
We did not notice when rain stopped striking
the skylight but glance up at a crack that
runs through the glass. "Yum!" a twenty-year-old
exclaims, pours milk onto cornflakes, snot
smeared across his face, while his stepmother
convulses, breaks into sobs. We place hoops
around peonies so that growing buds will not bend
stalks to the ground. I search for swaying lines
of ants, but nothing is there; I survey irregular
white trunks of aspens, but nothing is there.
As *that* swivels into *this,* I thread a tiny
screw to fasten the bracelet around your wrist;
you pull back a wooden slat to open the gate.

Solstice Quipu

Hong Kong 87, New York 84;
he studies isobars on the weather map;

ashes accumulate at the tip of an incense stick;

mosquitoes are hatching near the Arctic Circle;

300,000 acres in Arizona scorched or aflame;

the aroma of *genmai* tea from a teapot with no lid;

where is the Long March now?
And Lin Biao — so what if
he salivated behind a one-way mirror at naked women?

lobstermen color code their buoys;

string sandals number knotted mine the gold of the output of s on —
though things are not yet in their places,
the truth sears his fingertips:

the output of gold mines,
the number of sandals knotted on string;

orange globe of sun refracted through haze;

a two-year-old gasps at hummingbirds lying on a porch;

he notes a torn screen, nods
male and *female, black-chinned;*
spells the iridescent gorget of spring.

Inflorescence

Go sway on a suspension bridge over a gorge;
you do not ponder the beauty of an azure
lotus-shaped wine-warming bowl with five
spurs the size of sesame seeds at the base,
but, instead, inhale the cool mist sliding
over pines, making the white boulders below
disappear and reappear. This is how you
become absent to pancakes smoking on a griddle –
pricked once in thought, you are pinned,
singed back to the watery splendor of the hour:
wisteria leaves thin to transparency on the porch;
a girl relaxes on horseback in the field
while sunlight stipples her neck. You smile,
catch the aroma of pumpkin seeds in the oven,
exult at the airy, spun filaments of clouds.
Before there was above and below, who was there
to query? One marks a bloody trail in water
from a harpooned narwhal, dreams of clustered
igloos lit by seal oil. You flicker, nod:
what one has is steeped in oil, wicked into flame.

2

Whisked back and forth,
a fly
drops on water;

      a floating narwhal
      resembles a human corpse;

screwdrivers, pliers, CDs,
a duct-taped taillight
strewn in the grass;

      running my tongue
      along your nape;

singed by
apple leaves
on the windshield;

      smooth black stones
      in a glass bowl;

where the mind
that is
no-mind is;

      fingertips
      on a frosted pane.

3

A shrinking loop becomes a noose: at the airport
a Choctaw writer scrawls a few words to his wife,
creases the paper, fires a slug into his chest.
A woman smokes, ruminates on a blank canvas
she does not yet know will remain blank.
I push hoops into the dirt, prop up a few
tomato branches: a single Black Krim has reseeded
from last summer. I uproot some weeds, toss them,
but, in thought, recoil from flies on a squirrel;
raise a lid to a plastic barrel: find hamburger
wrappers, stomped soda cans, irregular bits
of white glass near where I vacuum my car.
As a red snake snags its epidermis, the mind snags,
molts from inside out. Although sand plunges
in an hourglass – soon the last white particles
will vanish from the top – I ache for a second,
sulfur butterfly pinned over black paper, to stop:
but, eelgrass in tidal water, I catch the scent
of tomato leaves on my hands, swing palms near
a horse's head: flies flit and land, flit and reland.

4

Incise the beginning and end to all motion;

q w e r t y u i o p, in a line above your fingertips;

align river stones for a walkway;

halt at clusters of notes from swinging copper-green wind chimes;

shovel twigs and beer cans out of a ditch;

this wave of pollen light on your face is the end of summer;

rub Maximilian sunflower petals with your hands;

sniff red silk pine-bark patterned gauze unearthed out of a tomb;

splay juniper with an ax;

water brims her eyes when you stroke her wrist;

a *Bombyx mori* consumes mulberry leaves for seven days;

ponder a missing shade of blue;

sweat when you eat that Chimayo chili stuffed with lamb;

graze patches of faint aquamarine paint on a bathroom door;

revolve a polygon inside a circle;

squint up at a magpie nest in the cottonwood branches;

survey a skater's mark left on the ice in executing a half-turn;

inscribe the beginning and end to all motion.

In the zero sunlight a man at a traffic light
waving today's newspaper becomes a man
who, wiping windshields at night in a drizzle
as cars come off the Brooklyn Bridge,
opens his hands. Behind your parked car,
you stoop to peruse a speckled brown egg
on the gravel, glance up to sight a ring-tailed
lemur on a branch. Though no red-winged
blackbirds nest in the cattails this summer,
though someone has tried to drain the pond
into a nearby acequia, there is nothing
to drain, and you nod, curse, laugh –
you have nothing, everything in mind.
When I run my fingers between your fingers,
when we wet river wet through white Embudo water,
the hush is a shocked stillness: a black
bug stretches the skin of water and circles out.
As moonlight slants through the screen door,
I mark the span of our lives suspended
over the undulating scritch scratch of crickets.

6

I sip warm wine out of a sky blue bowl
flecked with agate crystals in the glaze,

press my eyes, squint at walruses on an ice floe.
When you step on stones in plover formation

and enter a tea garden – shift the rhythm
of your body, mind; admire the slender

splayed arc of branches, singed maple leaves
scattered on gravel – you arrive at the cusp

where you push open a blue-planked door,
inhale the aroma of a miniature calla lily

in an oblong vase, bend over a brass trash can
to find a cluster of ants that must have

dropped from the ceiling and, disoriented, died.
And as the configuration at dusk of flaring

willow leaves on the skylight becomes minnows
in water, what is above becomes what is below.

And what appears up close to be a line
becomes by air, the arc of a circle.

7

A woman and an instructor skydive over an island;
their parachutes fail, and they plunge into a yard,
barely missing someone snipping morning glories.
How long did they free-fall before they knew
the end? We stare at Dungeness crab shells strewn
across the table, pull cupcakes out of the oven,
and, smoothing icing on them to the rhythm of
African drumming, sizzle along a cusp of dream.
Who knows what the Coal Sack in the Milky Way is?
Who cares that the Eta Carinae Nebula is about
9,000 light-years distant? A moment in the body
is beauty's memento mori: when I rake gravel in
a courtyard, or sweep apricot leaves off a deck,
I know an inexorable inflorescence in May sunshine;
watch a man compose a flower arrangement
in Tokyo using polychrome Acoma pots. And as
a narwhal tusk pokes out of a hole in the ice,
as a thumbprint momentarily forms in thawing frost
on a pane, we heat a precarious splendor,
inscribe the end and beginning to all motion.

Oracle-Bone Script

In oracle-bone script, the character for *attunement*
is a series of bamboo pipes tied together with string;
if only I had the words to make things that accord
in tone vibrate together. Sunlight streams between slats
of a fence onto the ground. I gaze across the field;
skunks have slipped into the neighbor's garden
and ravaged corn. At the mouth of an arroyo, someone
has drained engine oil into the sand, thrown quart
containers into the brush. "Goddamn," I whisper,
bending to pick cherry tomatoes, discover a large
grasshopper sunning on a branch. I imagine holding
a set of black-lacquered panpipes, blowing on them
for the first time in two thousand years. In the wobbly
beginning is a swish, then water trembling through bamboo,
tossed gravel, a dog's bark, throats slit, sleet,
footsteps, love-cries. I start as notes reverberate
in air; frost has shriveled the leaves into black bits.

The Welt

He longs for a day marked like a Song tea bowl
with indented lip and hare's-fur markings.

Yesterday they skirted two decomposing lambs
at the entrance to the big arroyo, covered

their mouths as they approached from downwind.
During firing, gravity pulls iron-oxide

slip down to form a hare's-fur pattern
on the glaze surface. They gagged at the stench,

saw pink plastic twine around the neck
of the mangled one by the post – he only wanted

to view it once. They moved on to the low-
voltage fence, looked for bison but saw none,

tried to spark the fence with a thrown stick.
He likes the plum blossom heat when

their bodies sway and thrash. They returned
along a smaller arroyo. In the aftermath,

cool to touch, a ghost of the body's heat.
In the morning they woke to sunburn on their necks.

In the Living Room

I turn this green hexagonal tile with
a blue dragonfly, but what is it I am turning?
The vertical scroll on the far wall

has seven characters that roughly translate,
"The sun's reflection on the Yangtze River
is ten thousand miles of gold." A Japanese

calligrapher drew these Chinese characters
in the 1890s, but who knows the circumstances
of the event? I graze the crackled paper,

recognize a moment ready to scrape into flame;
gaze at ceiling beams from Las Trampas,
at Peñasco floorboards softened with lye.

Along the wall on a pedestal, a gold-leafed
male and female figure join in sexual embrace.
Hours earlier, my hands held your hips,

your breasts brushed my chest. I close
my eyes, feel how in the circumference
of a circle the beginning and end have no end.

Acanthus

When you shut your eyes, you find a string
of mackerel tied by their tails over and across
the sloping street; pour water into raki
and watch it cloud into "lion's milk";
nibble smoked aubergine with yogurt;
point to red mullet on a platter of fish.
You catch the sound of dripping water,
squat to be near to the upside-down Medusa
head at the column base in a cistern:
a drop of water splashes your forehead.
You note carved acanthus leaves, then
eighteen women in singular postures
of mourning along the sides of a sarcophagus;
turn, at a noise, to bright lights:
eighteen men and women in security shirts
swarm through the covered street,
search for heroin. You smell saffron,
cardamom, frankincense, cinnamon, ginger,
galingale, thyme, star anise, fennel:
open your eyes to leeches in a jar
half-filled with water – green powdered henna
in a box alongside white mulberries.
The bells around the necks of goats clink;
you run your fingers along the fragments
of terra-cotta pots built into the stone
walls of houses; blink at the beggar
whose foot has swollen to the size
of his head; stagger up to Athena's temple
by moonlight; sit on a broken column,
gaze out across the gulf to Lesbos,
where lights glimmer along the curve
of a bay. In waxing moonlight, the water
is riffled, argentine, into wide patches.

You ache at how passion is a tangle
of silk in your hands, shut your eyes,
unstring the silk in one continuous thread.

The Thermos

Poppy seeds from a North Bennington garden
rest in white envelopes on a *granero*
in Jacona – to travel far is to return.
I am not thinking about the glitter of snow

on top of Popocatepetl, but how beauty
that is not beauty requires distance.
I recall the emerald gleam of glacier ice,
bald eagles perched at the tip of Homer Spit.

When I brought home that turtle-shaped
sandbox, we placed a giraffe, lion, tiger
at the edge. Sarah was happy to tilt sand
from her yellow shovel into a blue pail.

I scooped sand into a funnel and watched it
drain into the box. I do not know how
an amethyst crystal begins to take shape;
I do not know the nanoproperties of

silica or the origin of light, but I
know the moment a seed bursts its husk.
At work I spill tea out of a thermos,
smell your hair and how we quicken each other.

Ice Line

No one has slowed down
       and battered mailboxes
          at the junction;
at 2 A.M. a cricket
       periodically chirps
          in a corner of the bathroom;
earlier in the day,
       a horsefly bit
          into Sarah's back,
and her cry
       ululated in the air;
          later she peered at rain
in a Hiroshige print
       where men in bamboo hats
       leaned into
the relentless, slanting drizzle
       then pointed up at the skylight
       where raindrops
were pooled on glass;
       each night is a brimming
       pool of light,
and the contours are as
       intricate and shifting as
          the ice line around Antarctica.

The Chromatics of Dawn

Navel oranges ripen on branches near the steps
to a porch. He recalls zigzagging along a path

marked by white stones through a lava flow
to a beach where violet morning glories flared.

Up the coast he once peered into the water
but could not discern the underwater shrine

frequented by black-tipped reef sharks.
He tries to delineate the sheen of rolling waves,

chromatics to this hour when light pales
the unfolded paper shades to the south-

facing French doors. Last Wednesday they rolled
architectural plans, along with sun-bleached

red paper inscribed with gold characters,
and torched them in the hearth. As they remodel,

they ponder how a floor of repeating strips
of bolted oak and cement can be replicated;

but, at his fingertips, he knows nothing
can be replicated: neither the hair in her hairbrush,

nor the hole in his sock, neither the hue
of sunrise, nor waves of opalescent spring sleet.

Thermodynamics

He tips hot water into a cup, stirs the powdered
Ling Chih mushroom, hands it to you. You observe
black specks swirling in the inky tonic: sip,
shudder, sip. It is supposed to treat neurasthenia,
dizziness, insomnia, high serum cholesterol,
coronary disease, rhinitis, asthma, duodenal ulcers,
boost the immune system. You scan the room,
catch crescendos and decrescendos to the flute
music on the stand, pick out the first character,
"Spring," written in official script on a scroll –
Warring States bronze mirrors lined up on stands.
You pick up the last strands of glistening jellyfish,
note speckled tracks of grease on the platter,
feel as if you are jostled in a small airplane
as it descends into cumulus clouds. In Beijing
a couple wanted to thank him for arranging
financial sponsorship of their son in America;
under the table, she rubbed her leg against his
and whispered she had tomorrow off from work;
but *tomorrow, lust, betrayal, delight, yesterday,*
ardor, scorn, forgiveness are music from empty holes,
and you wonder if the haphazard course of a life
follows a fundamental equation in thermodynamics.
He pulls Styrofoam out of a box and reveals
a two-foot-high human figure from the tomb of
the Third Han Emperor; the face and trunk are intact,
though arms and hands are gone. He bequeaths
it to you, though requests that you pass it on
someday to a museum. You nod, sip the cool tonic,
down a few last black specks at the bottom of the cup.

X and O

Someone flips a lit match off the road
near a cluster of cattails, takes
another swig of beer, presses on the gas;
the match is not specifically aimed
at you: you just happen to be there –
at a stop sign, in a parking lot,
on a ferry, at a terminal; as a lens
narrows sunlight to a point that blackens
into flame, go ahead, zero in, try
to x out a ball of jasmine sprig
that unfurls in boiling water, x out
a red-tailed hawk shifting on a cottonwood
branch at dusk, x out coyotes yipping
as they roam by new moonlight up the road,
x out the dissolving suture threads
in your mouth, x out a dog's bark,
a baby magpie fallen from a nest
wandering on gravel, x out a flicker
feather in the mud; you can't x out
diarrhea, x out a barn erupted into flames,
x out firefighters lined up in trucks
along Russian olives, x out the charred
grass and stubs of fence posts, x out
a pang, place of birth or time of death,
x out, at an intersection of abscissa
and ordinate, dark matter that warps
space and time; you can't x out a cloud,
so make a lens of it the next time
you chop cilantro at a counter, the next
time you push through a turnstile.

The Angle of Reflection Equals the Angle of Incidence

Take that and that and that and that and –

a kid repeatedly kicks a dog near where
raw sewage gurgles onto sand at low tide,

Málaga, 1971. A man rummaging in a ravine
of trash is scrunched by a bulldozer.

If only I had q or r or s dissolves

into floaters in her eyes. Simmer. Scattered
ashes on blue-black Atlantic waves bob

and tinkle in the rippling tide of morning.
How quickly at dawn one makes out power lines,

cloud, fence, blue awning, orchard, plank

over ditch, but twisting chimney smoke
incites one to mark white apple blossoms

by a low gate, whale bones in a backyard,
chili roasting in a parking lot, or the memory

of wrapping an exposed pipe, the sizzle

when our tongues meet. When dead leaves
flowed downstream and encountered a sword,

they were razored in two. One, two,
four, eight: surmise a molten sword has

32,768 pounded layers before a final hissing.

Who believes what is written will never perish?
In 1258 Mongols hurled books into the Tigris

River and dyed the water black with ink.
Although a first record tabulating sheep and goats

has disappeared from a museum, the notation is

never expunged but is always renewed, amplified,
transmogrified. When a woman gives you a sheet

of handmade magnolia paper with mica flecks,
you lift it up to light, a milk snake's

translucent skin slides off. Though a strand

of silk unfurls to become a kilometer long,
tracks are not the only incubator of dreams.

So you missed the Eta Aquarid meteor shower,
or last week's total lunar eclipse. When you

sweep cobwebs out of the fireplace, sneeze,

scrutinize the veins of a peony leaf, you mark
the vertiginous moment of your beginning,

catch and release what you cannot hold,
smell kumquats in a glass bowl, stare down

at hundreds of red ants simultaneously fanning

out and converging at a point of emergence.
After a motorcycle blares past the north window,

the silence accretes: a rose quartz crystal
in the night. I garner the aroma of seared

scallops on a bamboo skewer; the ashes of

the woman who savored them scattered on waves.
Can watermelon seeds germinate in this moonlight?

The hairbrush, soap, thermometer by the sink
form a moment's figure that dissolves

as easily as an untied knot. A plumber fluent

in Sanskrit corrects my pronunciation of *dhyāna*,
while he replaces a chrome faucet fixture.

I pore over a cross-sectional drawing of a plum;
is an infinitesimal seed at the cross-

sectional center of the cosmos? Though a vibrating

crystal can measure increments, time itself
is a black thread. I arrive at a vernal cusp:

the murmur you make on the tide of sleep;
the sleighlike sounds when we caress.

Who waits and waits at a feeder for yesterday's

indigo bunting to arrive? A woman curls grape
roots into a sculpture, mentions her husband

died three years ago. We do not shut the eyelids
of the deceased, nor are we tied in quinine-soaked

sheets for delineating the truth. Once you begin,

the branching is endless: miller moths spiral
against a screened porch; we apprehend the shadows

of leaves on leaves, regard a goldfinch
feeding outside a window, a sparrow that keeps

flinging itself into glass. When a minute stillness

is sifted out of the noise, a whirlpool becomes
a spiral galaxy. When I run my tongue along

your clavicle, we dig clamshells out of the sand,
net red crabs at low tide. In the wren song

of brief rain, what matters is that we instill

the darkness with jade, live clear-eyed incising
a peony-blossoming dawn. And as someone trans-

plants bell peppers and onions into a garden,
leaves on a stream approach another sword

but, when they are about to touch, are repelled.

Quinoa simmers in a pot; the aroma of cilantro
on swordfish; the cusp of spring when you

lean your head on my shoulder. Orange crocuses
in the backyard form a line. *Once* is a scorched site;

we stoop in the grass, finger twelve keys with

interconnected rings on a swiveling yin-yang coin,
dangle them from the gate, but no one claims them.

Our meandering intersects with the vanished
in ways we do not comprehend: as a primary cord

may consist of two-ply two-color s-plied cords

joined by z spiraling single-colored simple cord:
I note the creaking cottonwood branch overhead;

moon below Venus in morning twilight; in our arms
one season effloresces into another into another.

The polar ice caps of Mars advance and retreat

with their seasons. Sometimes in gazing afar,
we locate ourselves. We were swimming in a river

below a sloping waterfall; I recalled wandering
away from the main peony garden and pausing

in front of blue poppies. To recollect is to

renew, invigorate, regenerate. A papyrus shoot
spikes out of a copper tub. *Hang glider, sludge,*

pixel, rhinoceros horn, comb, columbarium,
wide-angle, spastic, Leica lens, pincushion –

these have no through-line except that all

things becoming and unbecoming become part
of the floe. When I stare at a photograph

and count two hundred sixty-five hazelnuts,
examine the irregular cracks in their shells,

I recognize fractures in turtle plastrons,

glimpse the divinatory nature of language.
And as a lantern undulating on the surface

of a black pool is not the lantern itself,
so these synapsed words are not the things

themselves but, sizzling, point the way.

Earthstar

Opening the screen door, you find a fat spider
poised at the threshold. When I swat it,

hundreds of tiny crawling spiders burst out.
What space in the mind bursts into waves

of wriggling light? As we round a bend,
a gibbous moon burnishes lava rocks and waves.

A wild boar steps into the road, and, around
another bend, a mongoose darts across our headlights.

As spokes to a hub, the very far converges
to the very near. A row of Siberian irises

buds and blooms in the yard behind our bedroom.
A moth flutters against a screen and sets

off a light. I had no idea carded wool spun
into yarn could be dipped and oxidized into bliss.

Once, hunting for chanterelles in a meadow,
I flushed quail out of the brush. Now

you step on an unexpected earthstar, and it
bursts in a cloud of brown spores into June light.

Didyma

Disoriented, a woman wanders in the riverbed
east then west then east, asks us how to get
to County Road 101G. We stare at vertebrae
and long bones that protrude out of her plastic bag,
discern how one day the scavenger will become
the scavenged. At thirteen you dipped leaves
into melted wax in an aluminum pan on a stove,
had an inkling that in order to seal the shapes
you had to asphyxiate the leaves. And as
the area of your knowledge grew, the circumference
of your ignorance was always increased. You had
no idea you would live to recall so many deaths,
that they would become spots along a Pacific
coastline where you would come to gather salt.
You yearn for the ocean spray to quicken your eyes,
yearn for the woman you love to sway and rock.
When she sways and rocks, you sway and rock;
when you sway and rock, she sways and rocks;
when you convulse together, it is not hallucinatory
but a splendor that scavenges days and nights.

The shortest distance between two points is a straight line;

"Slob!"

red salamanders spawned in the Tesuque River;

an ocelot placed a paw on his chest while he slept;

he slapped a mosquito between his hands;

the position of beads on the abacus represented nyctalopia;

asphyxiated in a hotel room;

water in the black rubber bucket froze and never thawed;

red-winged blackbirds congregate in the cattails;

when he closed his eyes, she was there;
when he opened his eyes, she was there;

was afraid to cut the deck;

mosquito larvae quiver the water in the barrel;

rubbed her nipples;

sighted a rhinoceros in the crosshairs and went blind;

rearranged a tangram into the shape of a butterfly;

                    when he took off his glasses,
        oncoming headlights became volvox floating on black water;

            slashed the waves with ten thousand whips;

sunlight erased blue thumbprints but left the graphite lines unscathed;

                "The earth rests upon water."

3

What can be described can happen, he thought,
and visualized an ice cube sliding through a cup,
water passing through two slits in a wall:
quantum mechanics in the ensuing pattern of waves.
An hour after they ingested psilocybin mushrooms,
he lifted a cantaloupe in the garden, beheld
its weight, started at the intricate fretwork
on its skin; she touched a peach leaf, recalled
when she wrapped the first peach in white cheesecloth,
the juice on their fingers as they each ate half.
She pinched off tips of budding basil plants
and savored the aroma under her fingernails;
a heron landed near the top of a cottonwood,
but though he half expected a cry none came.
They poured and rubbed oil onto each other's skin;
their sighs and groans made the air tremble,
roil. They erased the plum bruises of a day,
restored themselves at a still point in the waves.

4

Green tomatoes on the windowsill:
if they are exposed to sunlight, will they ripen?

thud: a sparrow flies into kitchen glass;

they planted tulips on the slope behind the kitchen;

"Punks!"

he liked the digging;
she liked the slight weight of a bulb in her hand;

patter of rain on skylight;

they would forget the precise locations
but be surprised in spring;

at the stop sign,
who slowed and hurled a rock through the window?

as simple as a wavelength;

slivers of glass on the sofa, pillows, rug;

it is impossible to know precisely the velocity and position;

by the time you know the brightest yellow of a cottonwood leaf,
it's somewhere else;

yellow hawthorn leaves on the walkway;

shiver, shiver, shiver, shiver, shiver;

who walked from Miletus to Didyma?

he closed and opened his eyelashes along her ear.

5

A point of exhaustion can become a point of renewal:
it might happen as you observe a magpie on a branch,
or when you tug at a knot and discover that a grief
disentangles, dissolves into air. Renewal is not
possible to a calligrapher who simultaneously
draws characters with a brush in each hand;
it occurs when the tip of a brush slips yet swerves
into flame. A woman offers jasmine, dragonwell,
oolong teas: I inhale the fragrances, sip each one,
see chickens in stacked cages, turtles in tanks.
A man hosed blood off speckled white floor tiles
as we zigzagged toward the restaurant; over lunch,
I thought I heard moans and shrieks; when we left,
I glimpsed two white rabbits hauled by their necks
to a chopping block. The glint of the momentary
might dissolve like snow on water, or it might
burst into flame: yellow incense sticks smoking
in a cauldron, a large thin jasper disk that glows
like a harvest moon, the warmth in a glassed garden,
the way our daughter likes to rub foreheads.

6

Cr-rack! She stopped sewing when she heard the rock
shiver the glass window into shards, then the car
revved and sped up County Road 84 into darkness.
The moments you are disoriented are moments
when ink splatters onto the fibers of white paper.
As the area of your ignorance grows, it is possible
the circumference of your knowledge is increased.
Months after a brain aneurysm, when a man whispers
to his wife, "Nothing you do can ever make me happy,"
she turns to the midnight and sobs. When Xerxes
ordered his army to slash the waves of the Hellespont,
he slashed his own fingers to the tendons. Today
we gaze across the Dardanelles – whitecaps on teal water,
a few freighters zigzag down from the Black Sea.
Sunlight flares at the edges of leaves; heat ripples
up from the noon street and from rusted car tops.
The salt in the air stings my eyes: I lift a latch,
step into a patio: bird-of-paradise in bloom;
but, approaching the window, I find peeled paint,
cobwebs; it's dingy inside. I turn, wade into sleep.

7

"Do-as-you're-told scum sucker, you're the reason there are hydrogen bombs,"
yelled at the postal worker
behind the counter –

it leopards the body –

cringes at strangled
anteaters and raccoons hanging in the market –

it leopards the body –

wakes to pulverized starfish in his shoes –

it leopards the body –

disinterred a man and woman
sealed for 1,855 years
under jade plaques stitched with gold thread –

it leopards the body –

winced at hundreds of cicadas stridulating in the umbrella pines –

it leopards the body –

placed a blackbird with a red gash in the trash bin –

it leopards the body –

catches lamb shank in the smoke –

it leopards the body –

recovers a red tulip from inside a corkscrew dream –

it leopards the body –

combusts when they candlelight touch –

it leopards the body –

cars clunk
as they drive off the ferry at Çanakkale.

8

You walk up the steps and find a double peristyle
with a deep entrance porch filled with columns;
at the base of the columns is an octagonal set
of carved dragons, mermaids, and palmettes.
You turn, stride down a dark and narrow vaulted ramp
that emerges with blinding light into a large hall
open to the sky; a continuous frieze on three walls
has a central acanthus flanked by griffins and lyres.
At the far end, roped off by string, is the foundation
of an inner temple with steps that drop to a spring;
when you walk toward this sanctum and look back,
you see stairs to the platform of epiphanies at the rear.
You gaze up to the top of a sixty-five-foot column,
step up to the cord but can't get near enough
to see if the spring is dry or wet. You hunger
for insight into the precarious nature of becoming,
gaze at the woman you love, whet at how passion
is water from a spring, realize that yesterday,
exhausted, you were not going to come this far,
but today, having come, you have sunlight in your hands.

9

Because one stirred the entrails of a goat immolated on an altar,

because a magpie flicks tail feathers,

because blush-red tulips bloomed on the walkway,

because one speaks without fear of reprisal,

because a man – crushed in the debris of aluminum doors, steering wheel,
dashboard, shivered windshield – bleeds and moans,

because he had to visualize black petunias in order to spot Black Trumpets
on the forest floor,

because he slowly bites the back of her neck,

because an eagle glides over the courtyard with outstretched wings,

because a woman fasted, chewed laurel leaves, swayed in noon heat,
stammered *the here is always beginning;*

because she brushes her hair across his eyelids,

because bells tinkle around the necks of goats,

because the ruins of this moment are chalk-white dust in your hands,

because a grain of sand lodged,

because loss is a seed that germinates into *all things are full of gods,*

because a circle opens in all directions,

nine purple irises bloom in a triangular glass vase –

a pearl forms in an oyster –

she folds a prayer and ties it to a green cryptomeria branch –

threaded sponges are hanging in the doorway –

a slug crawls along a railroad tie –

a double bass upstairs suffused the house with longing –

silk tree leaflets fold up when touched –

waking out of her coma, she vowed, "I will dip my hands in ink and drag
        them across white mulberry paper" –

a hummingbird, sipping at a columbine, darted off –

red mullets thrash in the water –

one casts to the end of time –

she wore gold-hooped earrings with her black dress –

urn shards were incorporated into the stone walls of houses –

they swam in the Aegean –

blossoming yellow forsythia is the form and pressure of the hour.

Notes

Quipu: Although quipus are usually thought of in connection with the Incas, ancient quipus exist in Asian cultures as well. In China, one can use the phrase *chieh sheng chi shih*, which means "the memorandum or record of knotted cords," to refer to how Chinese writing evolved before characters were invented.

p. 5   *Lepiota naucina:* a mushroom that appears in grass and marks the beginning of autumn

p. 9   earthshine: sunlight reflected by the earth that illuminates the dark part of the moon

p. 21   omega minus: a negatively charged elementary particle that has a mass 3,270 times the mass of an electron

p. 23   *jarana:* in Mexico, a small folk guitar

p. 47   *genmai:* (Japanese) a combination of green tea and roasted brown rice

p. 54   *Bombyx mori:* silkworm

p. 58   Coal Sack: a dark patch of obscuring dust in the far southern Milky Way

p. 64   raki: (Turkish) an aniseed liqueur, which, with water, turns milky white

p. 66   *granero:* in the Southwest, a grain container

p. 69   *Ling Chih:* (Chinese) a mushroom that is reputed to provide health and longevity, the "mushroom of immortality"

p. 75   *dhyāna:* (Sanskrit) a fixed state of contemplation

p. 85   Didyma: the site of a Greek oracular sanctuary in Asia Minor which includes the remains of a temple of Apollo

p. 94   Çanakkale: the principal town, situated on the Asian side, at the narrowest point of the strait between Europe and Asia

p. 96   Black Trumpets: *Craterellus fallax:* edible funnel-shaped mushrooms

About the Author

Arthur Sze is a second-generation Chinese American who was born in New York City in 1950. He graduated Phi Beta Kappa from the University of California at Berkeley and is the author of eight books of poetry. His poems have appeared in numerous magazines and anthologies and have been translated into Chinese, Italian, and Turkish. He has taught at Brown University, Bard College, Naropa University, and is the 2004–2005 Elizabeth Kirkpatrick Doenges Visiting Artist at Mary Baldwin College. He is the recipient of many awards, including a Lannan Literary Award for Poetry, a Lila Wallace–Reader's Digest Writer's Award, a Guggenheim Fellowship, an American Book Award, and fellowships from the National Endowment for the Arts and the Witter Bynner Foundation for Poetry. He lives in Santa Fe, New Mexico, with his wife, Carol Moldaw, and daughter, Sarah, and is a Professor of Creative Writing at the Institute of American Indian Arts.

The Chinese character for poetry is made up of two parts: "word" and "temple." It also serves as pressmark for Copper Canyon Press. Founded in 1972, Copper Canyon Press remains dedicated to publishing poetry exclusively, from Nobel laureates to new and emerging authors. The Press thrives with the generous patronage of readers, writers, booksellers, librarians, teachers, students, and funders—everyone who shares the conviction that poetry invigorates the language and sharpens our appreciation of the world.

Major funding has been provided by:

The Paul G. Allen Family Foundation

THE **PAUL G. ALLEN FAMILY** *foundation*

Lannan Foundation

National Endowment for the Arts

Washington State Arts Commission

NATIONAL ENDOWMENT FOR THE ARTS

WASHINGTON STATE ARTS COMMISSION

For information and catalogs:

COPPER CANYON PRESS
Post Office Box 271
Port Townsend, Washington 98368
360-385-4925
www.coppercanyonpress.org

This book is set in Electra, created by American typographer and book designer W.A. Dwiggins in 1935. The book title is set in Monotype's digital version of Bulmer, originally cut by William Martin in 1790. Book design by Valerie Brewster, Scribe Typography. Printed on archival-quality paper.

—〰—